Earwig

Stephanie St. Pierre

Heinemann Library
Chicago, Illinois

Designed by Wilkinson Design
Illustration by David Westerfield
Printed and bound in Hong Kong

06 05 04 03 02
10 9 8 7 6 5 4 3 2 1

Library of Congress Cataloging-in-Publication Data
St. Pierre, Stephanie.
    Earwig / Stephanie St. Pierre.
        p. cm. — (Bug books)
    Includes bibliographical references (p.   ).
    ISBN 1-58810-172-X (lib. bdg.)
    1. Earwigs—Juvenile literature. [1. Earwigs.] I. Title. II. Series.
QL510 .S72 2001
595.7'39—dc21
00-012401

Acknowledgments
The author and publishers are grateful to the following for permission to reproduce
copyright material:
Cover: AGE/Peter Arnold, Inc.
p. 4 James H. Robinson/Animals Animals; p. 5 Photo Researchers, Inc.; pp. 6, 8, 14, 19 Hans
Pfletschinger/Peter Arnold, Inc.; p. 7 P. Ward/Bruce Coleman, Inc.; p. 9 R. N. Mariscal/Bruce
Coleman, Inc.; pp. 10, 11 Steve Hopkin/Ardea; p. 12 Corbis; p. 13 William Grentell/Visuals
Unlimited; pp. 15, 28 Jane Burton/Bruce Coleman, Inc.; p. 16 Nigel J. H. Smith/Earth Scenes;
p. 17 Crandall & Crandall; p. 18 Satoshi Kuribayashi/Oxford Scientific Films; p. 20 William E.
Ferguson/Visuals Unlimited; p. 21 AGE/Peter Arnold, Inc.; p. 22 Simon D. Pollard/Photo
Researchers, Inc.; p. 23 George D. Cepp/Photo Researchers, Inc.; p. 24 Mike Biakhead/Oxford
Scientific Films; p. 25 Gary A. Conner/Photo Edit; p. 26 Shepherd T. OSF/Animals Animals;
p. 27 Tim Shepherd/Animals Animals; p. 29 Tony Freeman/Photo Edit.
Special thanks to James Rowan for his help in the preparation of this book.

Every effort has been made to contact copyright holders of any material reproduced in this
book. Any omissions will be rectified in subsequent printings if notice is given to the publisher.

Some words are shown in bold, **like this**. You can find out what they mean by looking
in the glossary.

Contents

What Do Earwigs Look Like?

Earwigs are **insects.** Their bodies are made of three parts—a head, a **thorax,** and an **abdomen.** They have three pairs of legs and a wing case that covers one pair of wings.

Earwigs are small and flat. Most are about the size of a peanut. Earwigs are brown. Some have stripes. They have two long **antennae** and a pair of **cerci.**

What Are Cerci?

Earwigs have large pinchers called **cerci.** They are at the end of the earwig's **abdomen.**

Male earwigs have curved cerci. Females and young have straight cerci. The cerci are used to grab food. Sometimes they are used to fight other earwigs.

How Are Earwigs Born?

Earwigs **hatch** from eggs to become **nymphs.** A female lays 20 to 50 small white eggs at a time. She lays the eggs in a **burrow** in the ground.

The eggs that hatch together are called a **brood.** Earwigs usually have two broods in a season. One brood is born in early spring. The second brood is born at the end of spring.

How Do Earwigs Grow?

Earwig babies are called **nymphs.** They look almost the same as adults but are smaller. They are gray-brown. They do not have their wings yet.

It takes a few months for an earwig to grow up. When it is growing the nymph gets too big for its skin.

How Do Earwigs Change?

The **nymph** sheds its tight skin. This is called **molting.** Nymphs molt four or five times before they are fully grown. Finally the earwig reaches full size.

When the earwigs are fully grown they usually leave home. The mother earwig stops taking care of her grown babies. In fact, if they don't leave her, she may eat them.

What Do Earwigs Eat?

Earwigs eat moss, **fungi,** and **pollen.**
Most of the time earwigs eat plants.
They will also eat spiders. Sometimes
they even eat other earwigs.

Earwigs often eat flowers. In the summer and fall they eat fruit. They will eat honey out of a beehive if they can.

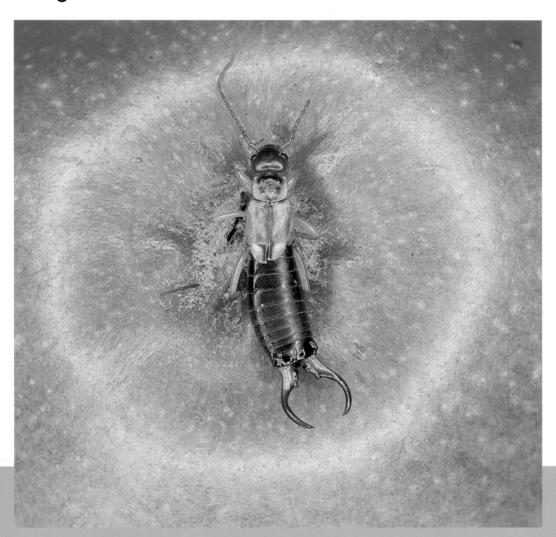

Where Do Earwigs Live?

Earwigs like **damp,** shady places. Most earwigs live outdoors. Outdoors you might find earwigs living in a woodpile, under a stone or fallen tree, or in a pile of leaves.

Some earwigs live inside. They hide in cracks near walls. They like **musty** spots in bathrooms or kitchens. They also live in damp places such as basements.

What Do Earwigs Do?

Earwigs cannot hurt people. Their **cerci** look fierce but they can only give a person a tiny pinch. Earwigs got their name because some people believed they climbed into people's ears. But this is not true.

Earwigs are **nocturnal.** That means they move around during the night and sleep during the day. At night earwigs come out of their hiding places and look for food.

How Do Earwigs Move?

Most earwigs have wings, but they do not usually fly. They move around by crawling. They are fast crawlers, but they can't go very far.

Earwigs climb up things like stems, sticks, or strings. They climb until they reach the top and then they stop. The earwigs will stay still at the top until something or someone moves them from their **perch.**

How Do Earwigs Travel?

Earwigs almost never fly. They cannot crawl very far either. But earwigs do travel over long distances by hiding in things that can move a long way.

Earwigs might get a ride to a new home by hiding in flowers. They might even get a ride in a car.

Which Animals Attack Earwigs?

Earwigs do not have many enemies. They do not taste good to birds or to most other **insects.** Some earwigs squirt a bad smell when they are in danger.

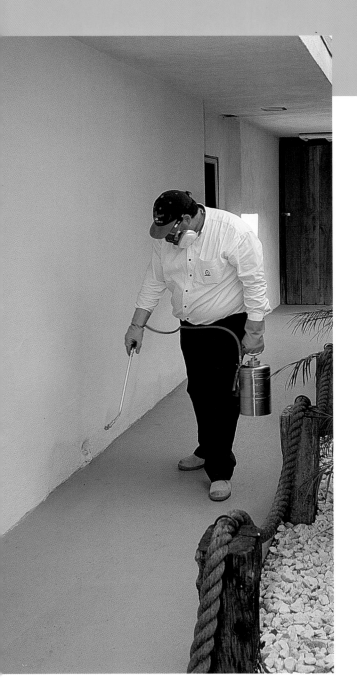

The biggest danger earwigs face is from people. People stomp them or spray them with poison. Earwigs also get sick and die from disease. Tiny worms and **parasites** can also hurt earwigs.

What Makes Earwigs Special?

Most **insects** do not care for their babies. But earwig mothers do. After she lays her eggs the mother watches over them until they **hatch.**

The earwig mother protects her babies from enemies. She keeps the **burrow** clean and brings food to the babies. This goes on for a few weeks.

Thinking about Earwigs

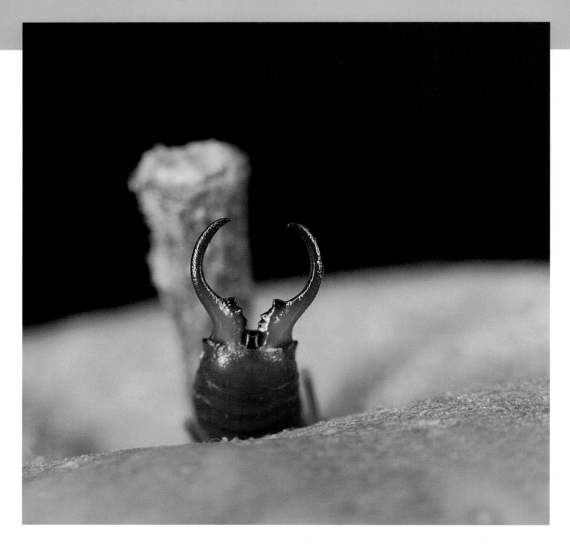

The earwig's **cerci** look dangerous.
How does the earwig use them?

Look at this picture and think about where earwigs might live. Would they live under the rocks? Or in the trees? Where do you think you would find them?

Bug Map

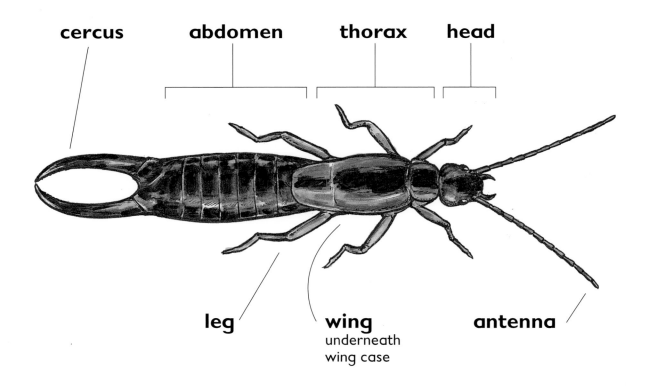

cercus   abdomen   thorax   head

leg   **wing**
underneath
wing case   antenna

Glossary

abdomen tail end of an insect

antenna (more than one are called antennae) long, thin tube that sticks out from the head of an **insect.** Antennae can be used to smell, feel, hear, or sense direction.

brood group of babies that hatch at the same time

burrow underground nest

cercus (more than one are called cerci) pincher at the insect's tail end

damp a little bit wet

fungus (more than one are called fungi) plant, such as mushrooms or mold, that cannot make its own food

hatch to be born out of an egg

insect small animal with six legs

molting shedding the old, outer layer of skin that has been outgrown

musty slightly wet and old-smelling

nocturnal animal that is active at night, and sleeps during the day

nymph insect baby that has hatched from an egg and looks like the adult insect with no wings

parasite animal that lives and feeds off of other creatures

perch place where an animal can rest and watch, usually up high

pollen yellow dust found on plants

thorax middle part of an insect's body, where the legs are

More Books to Read

Miller, Sara Swan. *Will You Sting Me? Will You Bite? The Truth about Some Scary-Looking Insects.* Owings Mills, Md.: Stemmer House Publishers, 2001.

Souza, Dorothy M. *Insects around the House.* Minneapolis, Minn.: Lerner Publishing Group, 1991.

Stewart, Melissa. *Insects.* Danbury, Conn.: Children's Press, 2001.

Index